My Cat
Loves
Me
Naked

Stephanie Piro

SOURCEBOOKS HYSTERIA™
AN IMPRINT OF SOURCEBOOKS, INC.®
NAPERVILLE, ILLINOIS

Published by Sourcebooks, Inc.

P.O. Box 4410, Naperville, Illinois 60567-4410

(630) 961-3900

Fax: (630) 961-2168

www.sourcebooks.com

ISBN-13: 978-1-4022-0736-0

ISBN-10: 1-4022-0736-5

Printed and bound in the United States of America

CH 10 9 8 7 6 5 4 3 2

Introduction

Hi. My name is Stephanie, and I'm a cat lady. I only have three cats, but that's because I am married. Otherwise, I'd own every cat I see in those sad adopt-me-and-take-me-home photos that pet shelters place in newspapers. I've been living with and drawing cats most of my life. They are great company and a constant source of inspiration and entertainment. I can see why women often prefer to live with cats. Your cat doesn't care what you look like naked. As long as you supply the food, he wouldn't notice if you were green and had a third eye!

Cats don't start fights, or yell at you, or stop talking to you for almost no reason at all. They don't leave hair in the sink (they do tend to leave it everyplace else), and they don't take up much room on the bed, unless you have more than a dozen. There *is* the issue of hairballs and mouse parts, but we will deal with that later.

Although men sometimes keep a lot of us from truly manifesting our inner cat ladies—the ones who want eight or nine cats or more—we cat ladies are very welcoming and not at all sexist. (I maintain that men can be cat ladies, too!) In fact, we love all men who open their hearts and homes to one or more cats. We salute you! And, if you're single, we may even have the purr-fect girl for you! Because we outnumber you (as far as we know), you are a valuable commodity in the cat lover community.

We women are nurturers by nature. We melt at the sight of babies, puppies, and other warm, cuddly, and adorable things, but show us a cat, especially a pathetic stray, and we go nuts! We want to shower it with love and affection and visits to the vet, which end up costing a month's salary. We spend hours thinking up the perfect name, which most cats then choose to ignore. We let it claw its way into our hearts, and once settled, it deigns to notice us when and where it chooses. When it comes to cats, women are the biggest suckers on the planet. And we love it!

I hope you enjoy this collection of some of my very favorite cartoons about cats and the women who love them.

"If men didn't exist...
women would have
a lot more cats!"

"Good morning!"

Just the two (or three or four) of us

The first thing many of us do when we get our own place is get a cat. Or, in some cases, a couple of cats. They're great company, low maintenance (mostly), and come in a variety of colors to match your wardrobe or décor.

Sharing your home and hearth with another creature often takes some adjustment. In fact, learning to live with cats prepares us for living with other species down the road, like husbands.

And remember, when all your friends avoid you after a bad break up because they're tired of hearing you complain, you have a captive audience at home. Your cat becomes your ally, your confidant. He or she will always be there to listen to your troubles, cheer you up, or give you a dose of reality by ignoring you. These cartoons celebrate that special bond between you and your cat.

"Who needs cushions when you have cats? Cushions don't purr!"

Stephanie

" You think I could lose a
few pounds!? My cat
doesn't think I'm fat !
My cat LOVES me naked!"

"And now, I will wash my hair! I never have a bath without an audience!"

"Why is it I'm the only one who has trouble sleeping around here...?"

"I don't know why my parents even pretend to call me...! It's YOU they want to talk to!"

"Looks like we had a frost
last night..."

"Your species has evolved
beyond waiting for boy friends
to call, hasn't it?"

"In, out, in, out... I wish
my life was that simple!"

Lessons in lethargy and the art of adoration

How simple our cat's lives seem when compared to our own. All they have to do is sleep, eat, and, on a strenuous day, play with a catnip mouse. We, on the other hand, have to cook (microwaving *does* count as cooking!), clean, do laundry, run to the store just to buy cat food, go to work, and try to have a social life.

It's no wonder we admire cats. We crave the ability to lounge around guiltlessly, while delegating menial tasks to a lower order of species. We all hope to come back next time around as our own cats. They were worshipped as gods, after all. And girls, we deserve nothing less after what we put up with in our current lives!

"I might get more dates if I had a cute little chihuahua instead of a 10 lb couch potato!"

" They love going out for a little air!"

"I didn't forget, Eli! I asked for paper instead of plastic when I bought the groceries!"

" Finished? Can I turn the page, yet?"

"I don't really own him... our relationship's based on mutual respect, so long as I provide the cat food!"

"Why do people think it's odd I have six cats? I think it shows great restraint on my part!"

"Come on in, and meet
the family!"

Love me, love my cat

So, you're living with your cat (or cats) and you think something might be missing from your life. A man. The search begins. You cruise the Internet, hit up friends for potential dates, scan the personals. And, one day, you hit the jackpot! You find the perfect guy! Things are looking good.

Except, you neglected to tell him about your current significant other (or others). It's time to break the news. No, not just to Mr. Right, but to Bootsie (and Pandora and Max). They have to learn to share you, the *food-god*, with someone who's going to hog your attention. Fortunately, despite jealous and possessive pussycats, some relationships do work out for everyone, providing more laps to choose from and extra tidbits from the table.

"Isn't that cute? Binky doesn't want to share me. He's territorial!"

"Hey guys! Mommy's brought home the bacon for another week... AND the cat food!"

Stephanie

"No idea who they are. They're my cat's friends."

"He's upset because you're drinking from his mug!"

"Oh, I forgot to tell you I'm rehabilitating feral cats, now!"

"You NEVER called! And NO, the cat didn't erase your messages!"

" You're the first man I've dated who's crossed the threshold. They usually don't make it past opening the door!"

"Aha!"

Can't live with 'em, can't live without 'em

Living with cats can be relaxing and stress reducing, as many doctors claim, with all that purring adding years to your life. On the other hand, sometimes cats are, shall we say, quite the handful. Did you luck out with the sweetest little fur muffin on the planet? Or do you share your home with Mr. Aloof, who hardly notices your presence, would rather die than sit on your lap, and if he does pay any attention to you at all, it's of the waiting-behind-the-couch-to-spring-into-action-and-attack-your-bare-feet sort?

Yet, you never give up, lavishing loads of affection on these sociopaths in hopes that they might one day see the light and realize how good they have it living with you—hopefully before any permanent scar tissue begins to form.

"She was always after the yarn... so, I taught her to knit... and there was no looking back!"

"All my furniture has the distressed look ... thanks to my decorator, Bebe, over there!"

"If you're through with the internet... I'd like to get back to work!"

"Excuse me, you may have 9 lives, but I only have 1 to try and get through!"

Stephanie

"Ah, forget waiting for Mr. Right! I know a litter of kittens that's just about ready for adoption!"

"Uh oh... I feel a hug coming on!"

"And you like yours, milk, straight up... hold the tea!"

You going to finish those chicken wings?

Cats on their own will survive on mice, grasshoppers, garbage, flotsam, and jetsam. But once they invade our homes, we discover we're living with the feline version of Emeril. They become picky. They sneer at store brands and generic labels. Get sick over fancy feline feasts in a can. What they want is what *you* are eating. Especially if that something involves chicken.

But, many cats are generous and want to take care of you, too. What cat lover hasn't woken up to find the gift of mouse gizzards on the rug or feathers under the table?

What could be more endearing?

" It's charades. Let's see...it flies, a bird? First syllable, tongue, no lick...? Sounds like licking?"

"You can't send it back to the chef. As far as I can tell from reading the label, there isn't one!"

"Just a heads up... you've been chowing down on the cat snacks!"

" There's an old saying: he who meows the loudest... gets the most chicken!"

Stephanie

"He's not allowed on the table... but he finds ways around that rule!"

" I hate opening a new bag of dry catfood, around here! Stop! No kibble diving!"

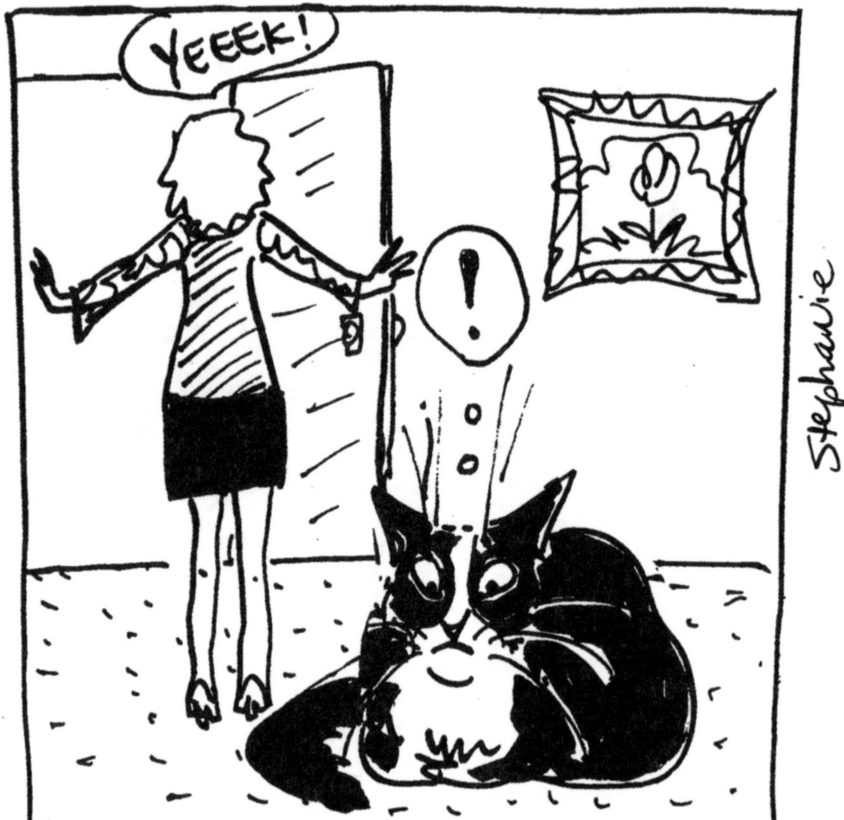
YEEEK!
!
Stephanie

"Oh, so that's where I left that mouse's head!"

"Like my new couch? The cat hair hasn't even settled yet!"

The many little bonuses to living with cats

Cats make their mark on your world in many diverse ways. Cat hair on the new couch, for example, can trigger a reaction from your new boyfriend whose love for you hinges on his ability to keep Claritin handy at all times. These things are good to know.

Then, of course, there is the delicate problem of the litter box. Whether to hide it, disguise it, or put it out for all to see. With your busy lifestyle, tending your cat's litter box sometimes has to take a back seat to things like primping for a big date. At such times, you may wonder how the car keys ended up on the roof of the garage.

Let's face it: we all know whose needs come first!

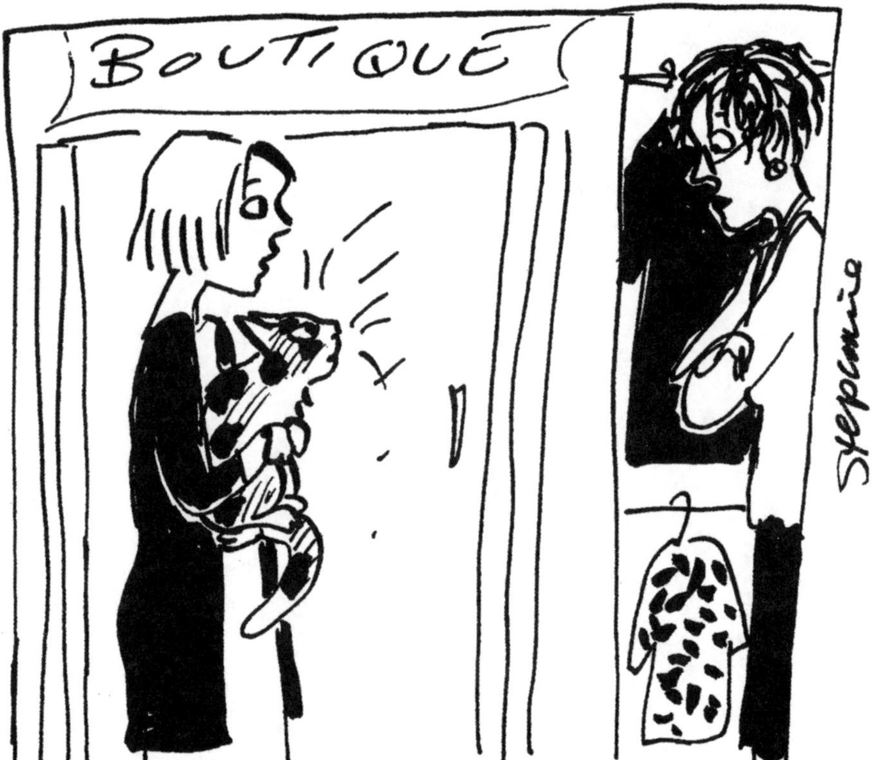
BOUTIQUE

"What do you have that matches my cat? I need a wardrobe that doesn't show cat hair!"

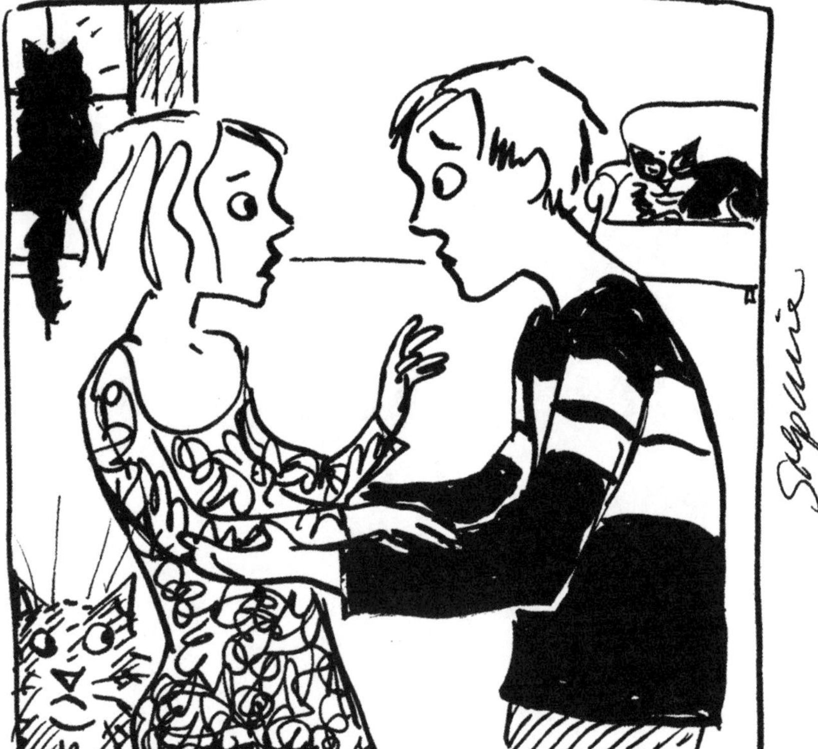

"You're the man of my dreams, except you're allergic to cats! I'll have to dream more specifically next time!"

"I can't be allergic to my cat! Could you run those tests again? Maybe it's my boyfriend?"

"Uh oh... I'm picking up the incriminating vibe of a not so clean litter box!"

"It's true what they say,
female cats ARE neater!"

"He needs his medicine 3 times a day. Canned food at 6. Dry food all day and clean water. Clean the cat box every day... You know, forget it! I'll just stay home!"

"Happy St. Patrick's Day to you, too... now, let it go!"

Happy Holidays!

Time to deck the halls and light the menorah. Having a cat means you never have to celebrate a holiday alone.

Stop worrying about the perfect party dress. Who needs a date for New Year's Eve when you've got a built-in buddy with his own tux and tails...um, tail. And Thanksgiving? Forget about that trek to your relatives where all anyone cares about is whether you're ever going to find an appropriate single man. You can stay home with someone who's truly thankful to be with you...*and* with all that turkey!

"Oh, look, Lisa's kitty sent you a Valentine! We'll have to send one to him, too, won't we?"

"one martini and one glass of milk in a martini glass, and would you mind singing "Happy Birthday, Muffy" when you bring them?"

"You didn't get me anything for Mother's Day. The least you could have done was caught me a mouse or something!"

"Gourmet food, kitty treats, tuna sandwiches... Quite the haul!"

" Great stuffing!"

"Look at that! We're Jewish! Mazel Tov!"

" You put a catnip mouse
in his stocking, again,
didn't you?"

Stephanie Piro is an award-winning syndicated cartoonist, designer, illustrator, and cat lover. Stephanie is one of King Features' landmark group of women cartoonists, the "Six Chix." Many of her illustrations have been licensed to calendar and greeting card companies. She and her newspaper editor husband and college student daughter reside in rural New Hampshire, where they share their home with three feline companions.

www.stephaniepiro.com
piro@worldpath.net